This Book Belongs To:..

....

....

....

COLOR TEST PAGE

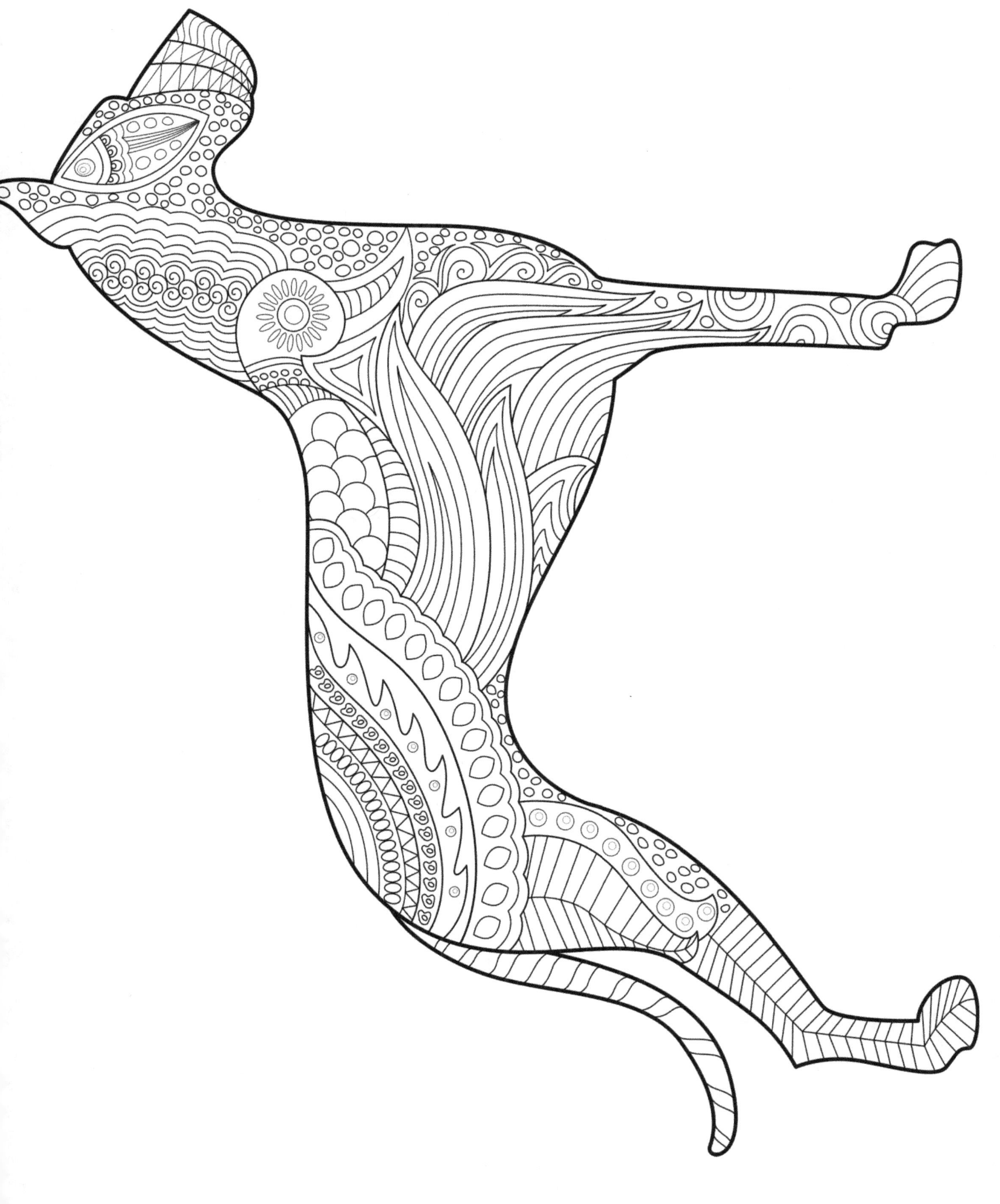

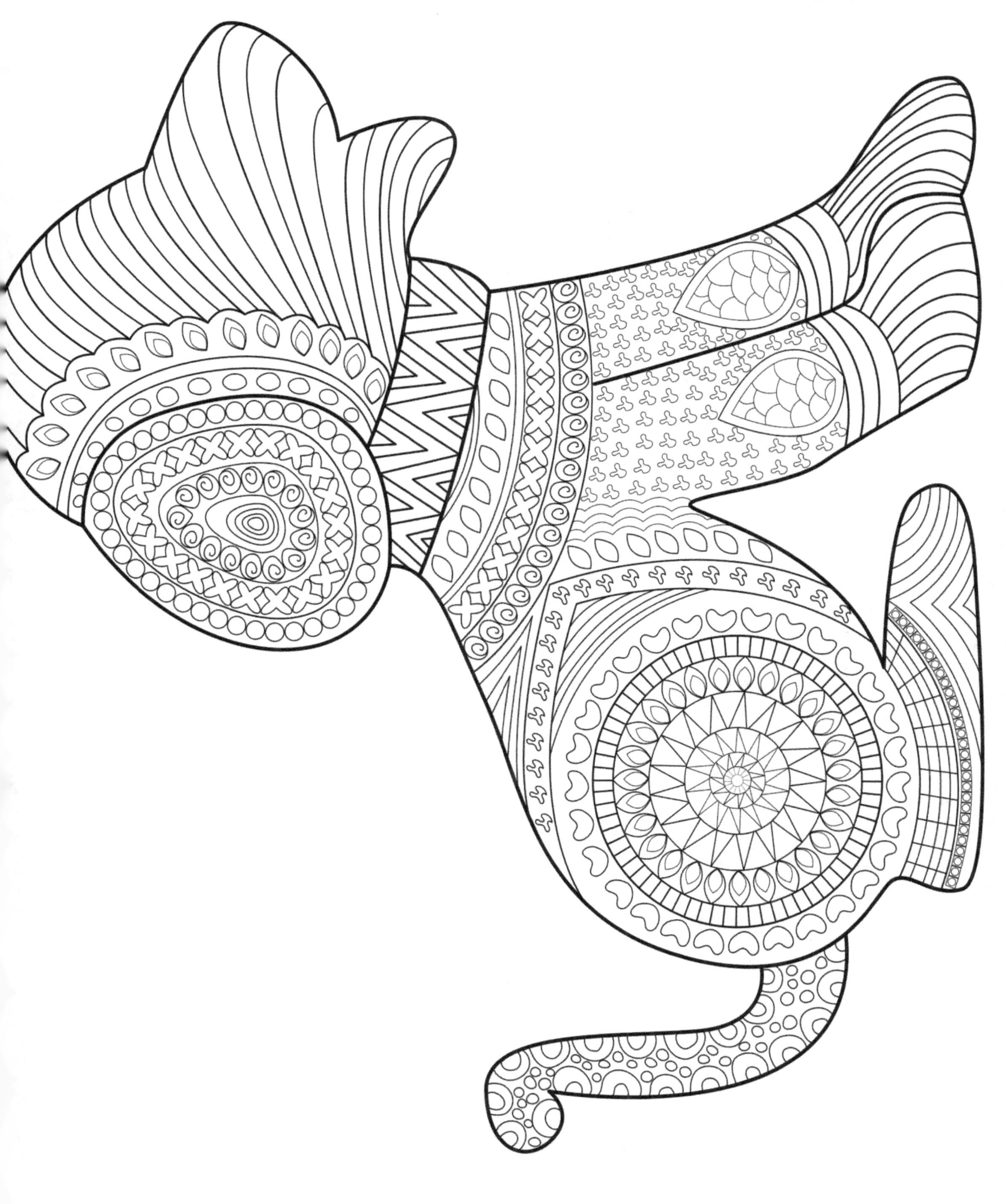

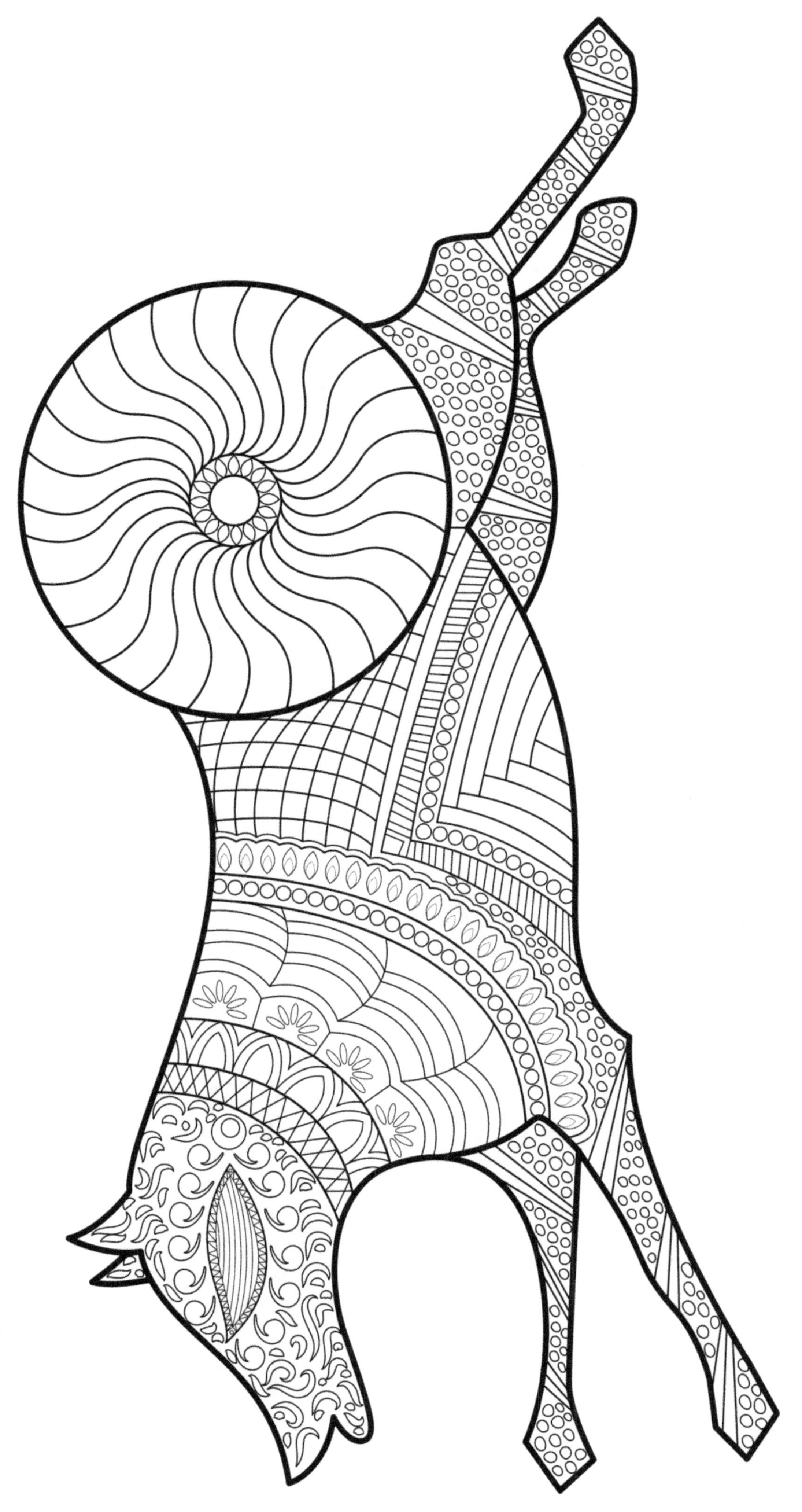

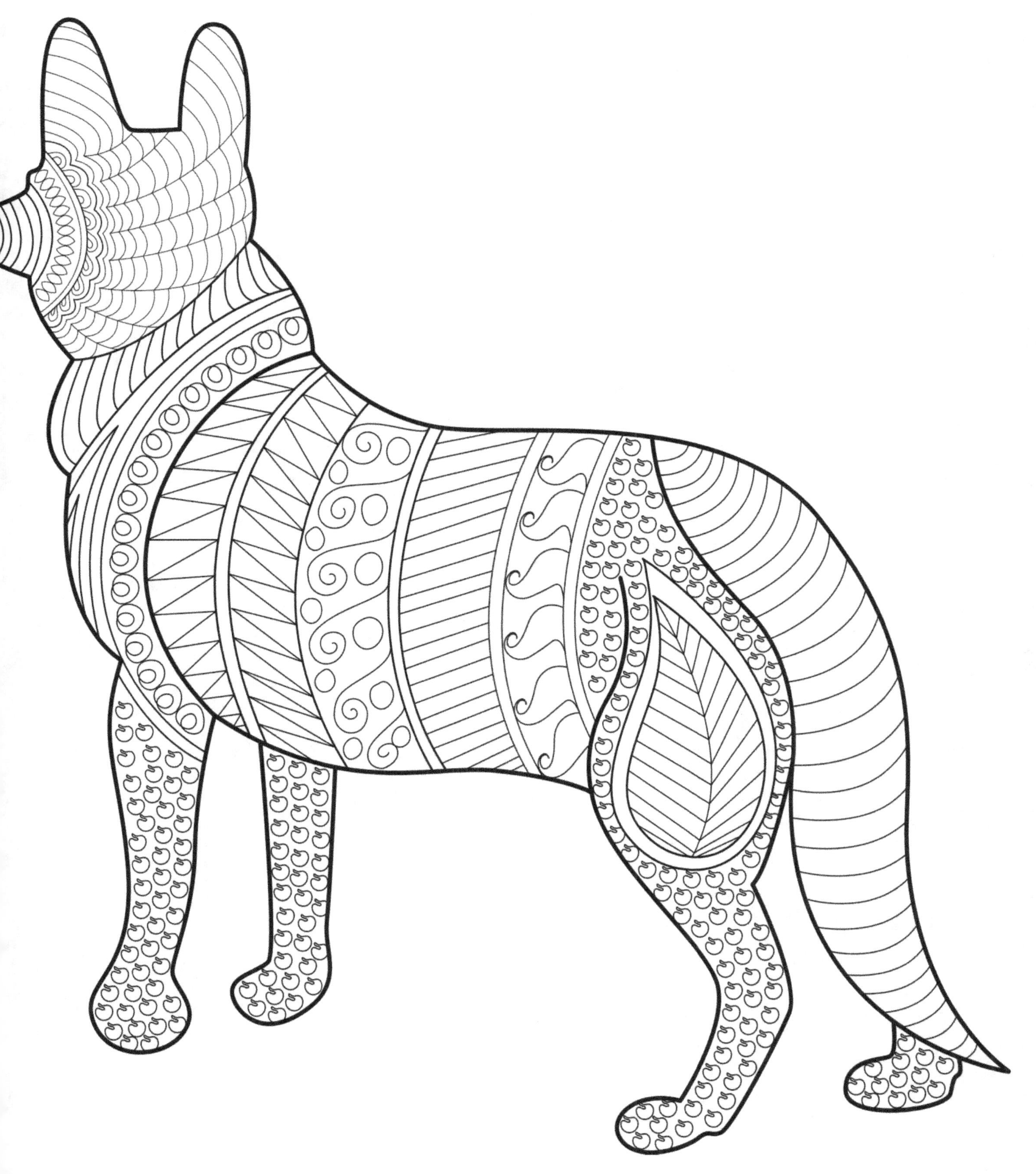

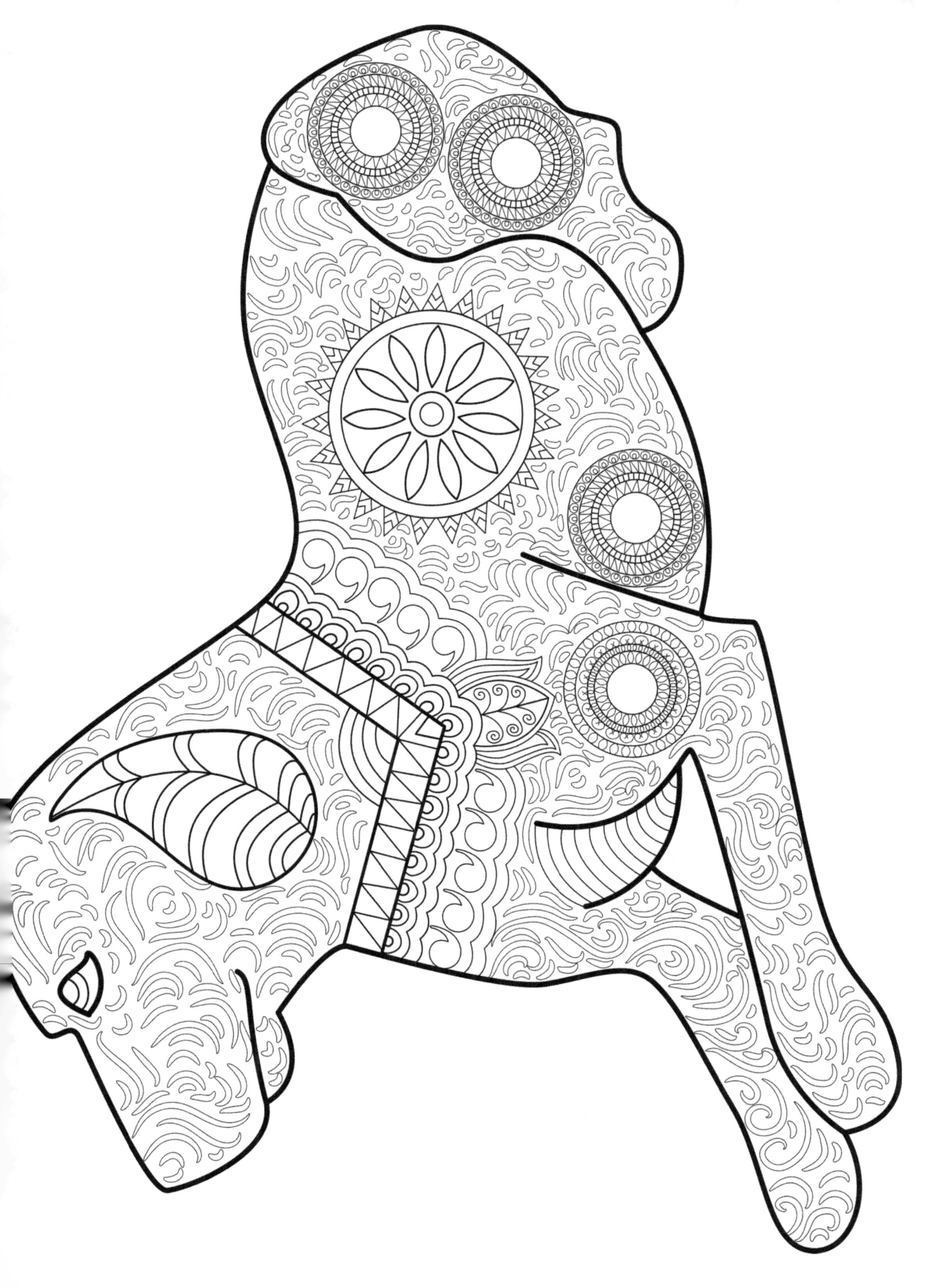

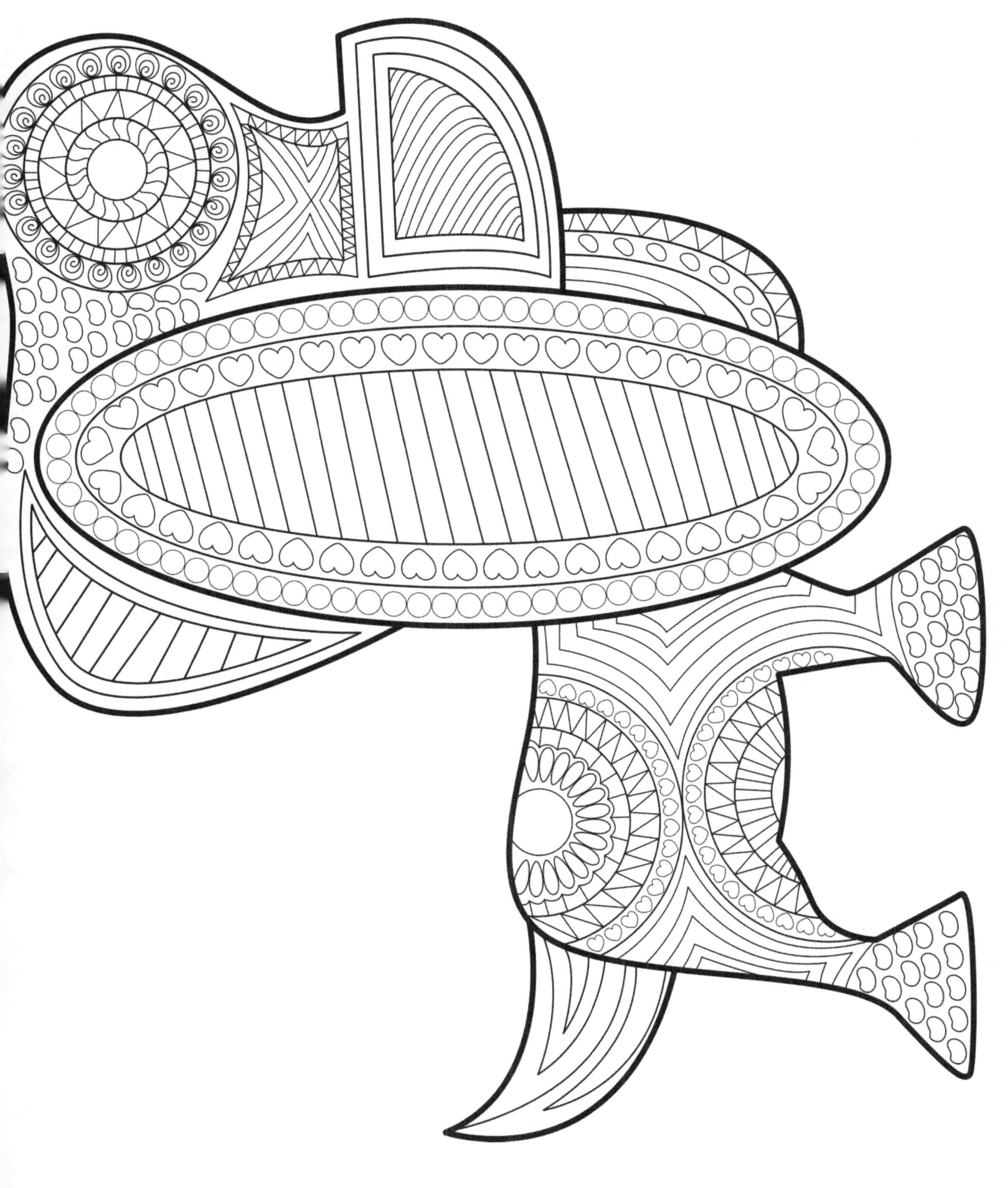

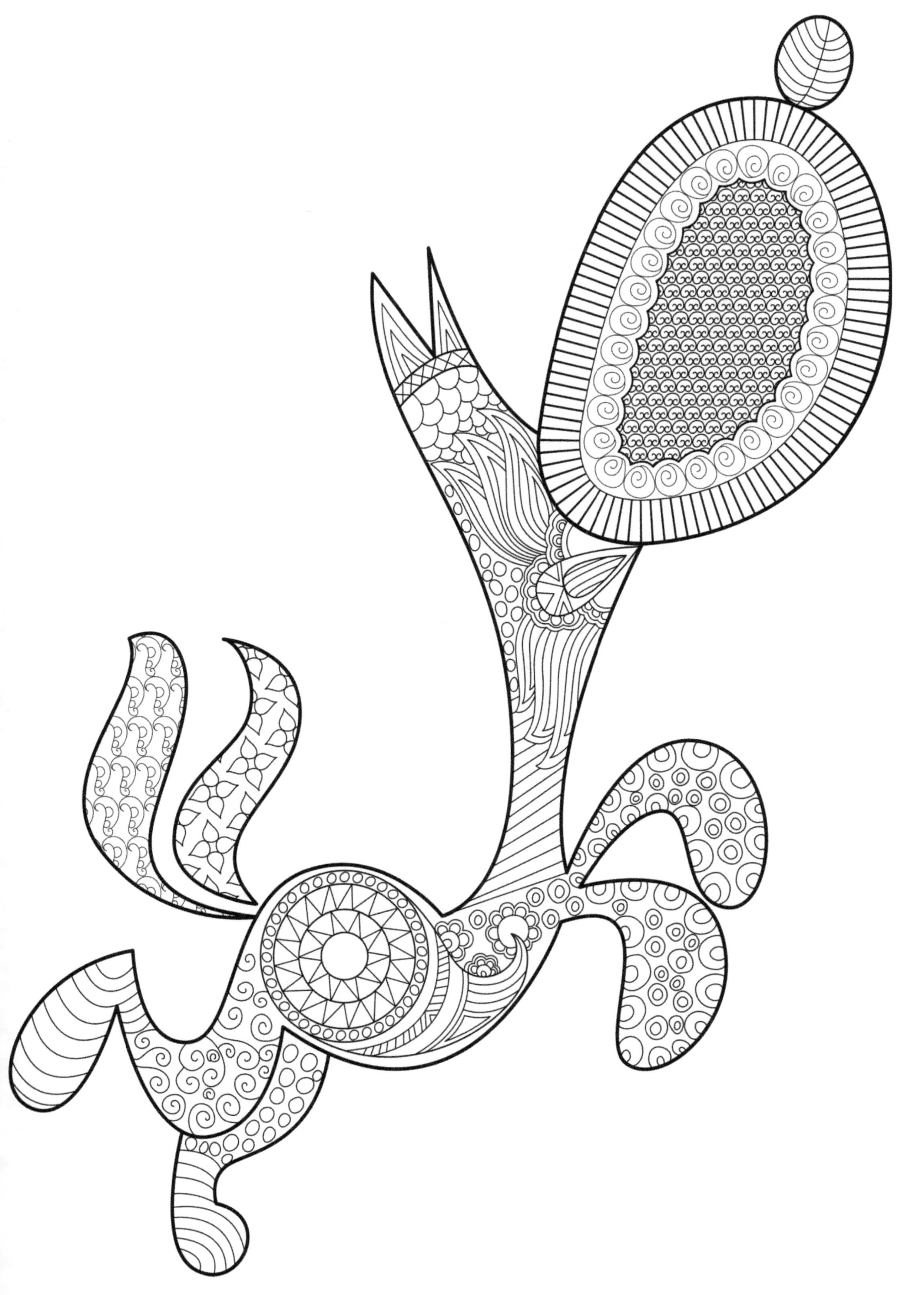

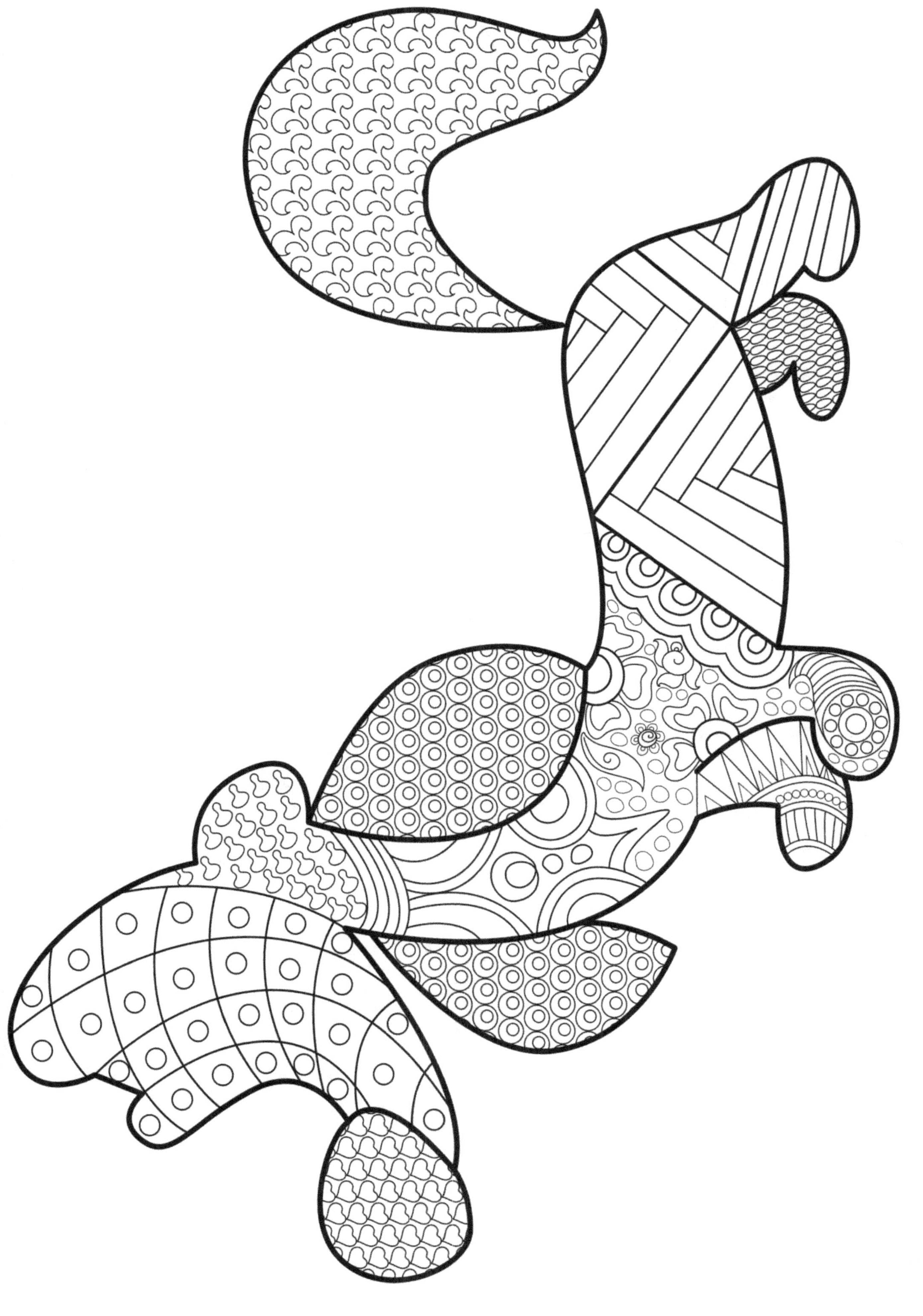

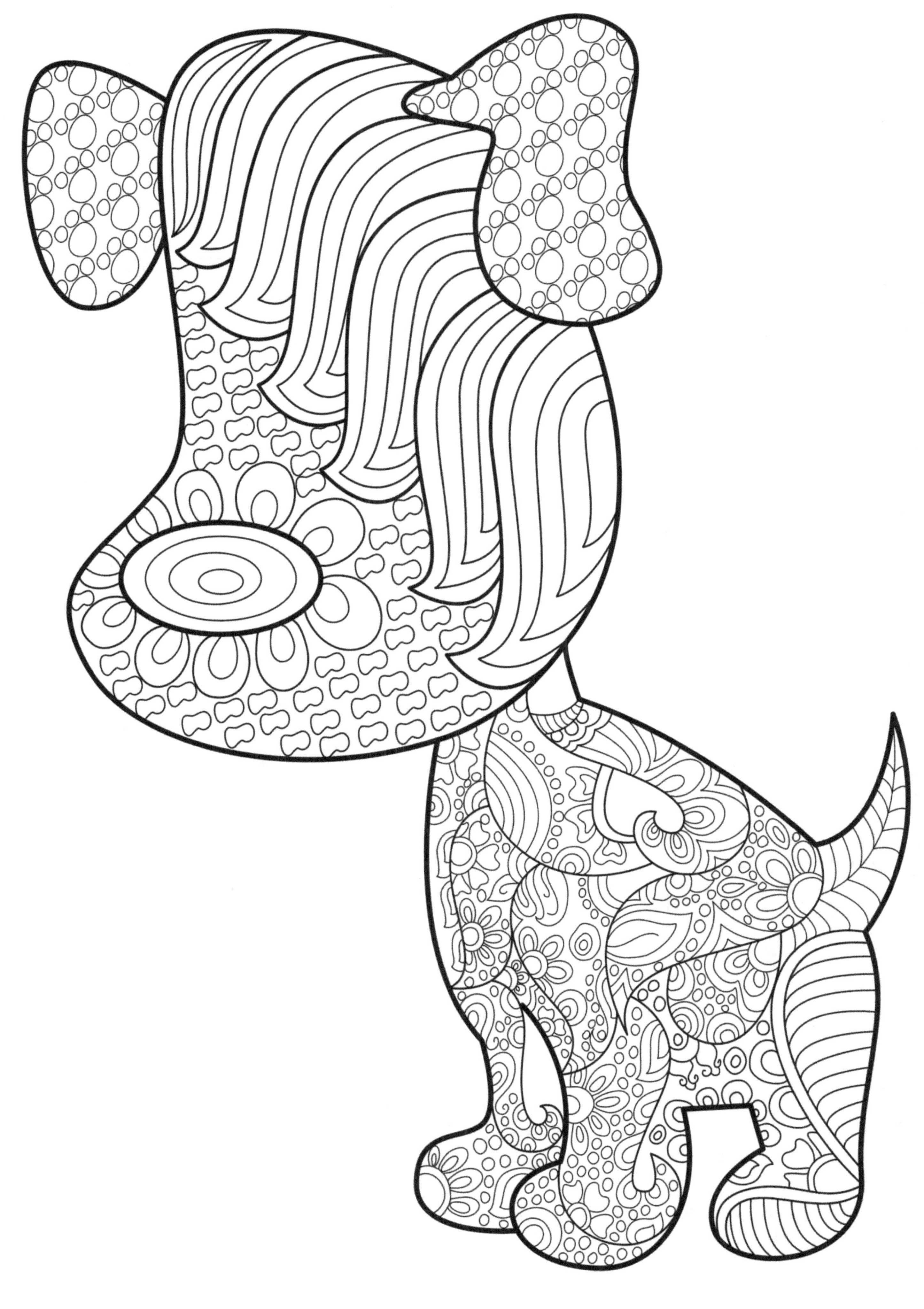

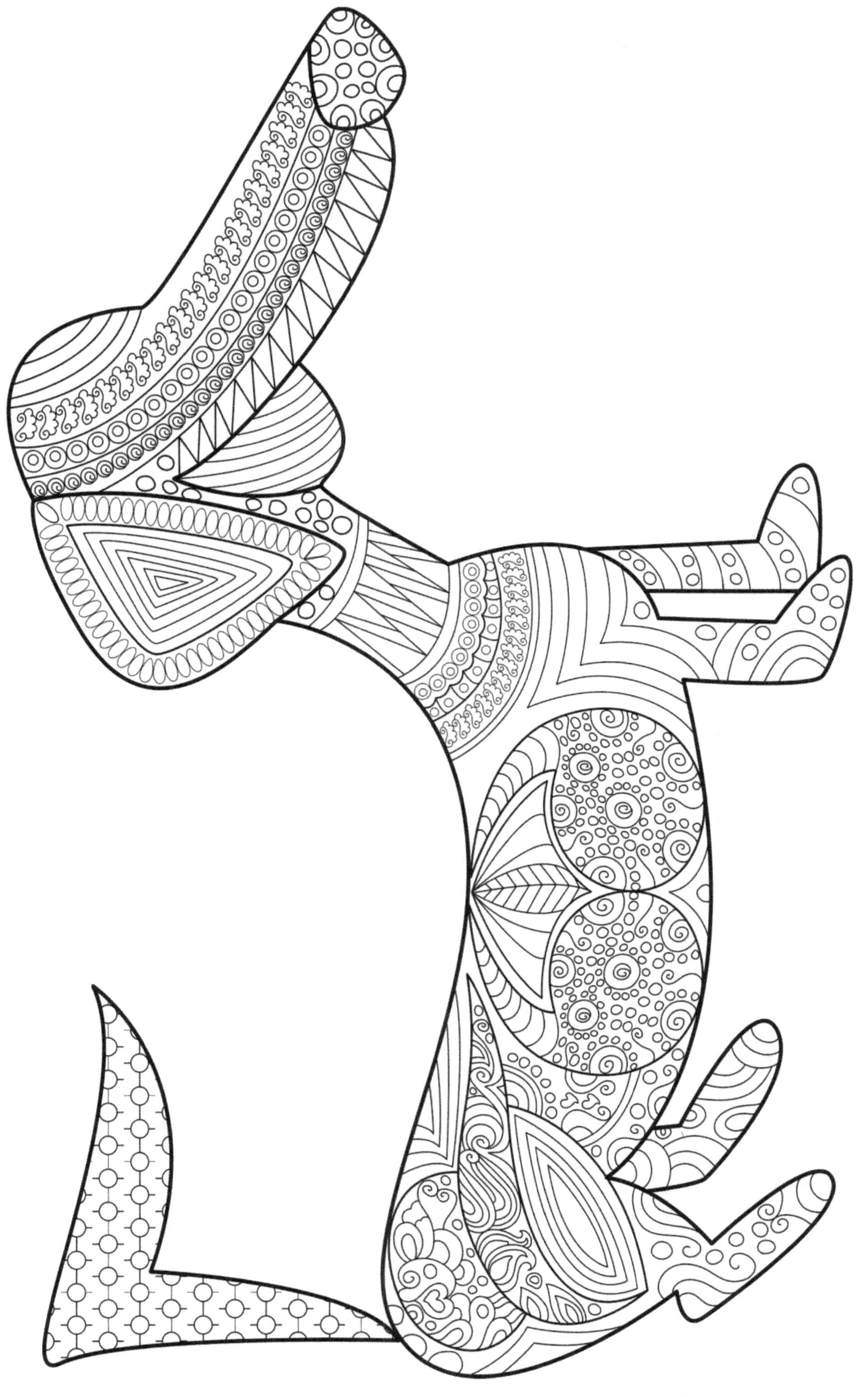

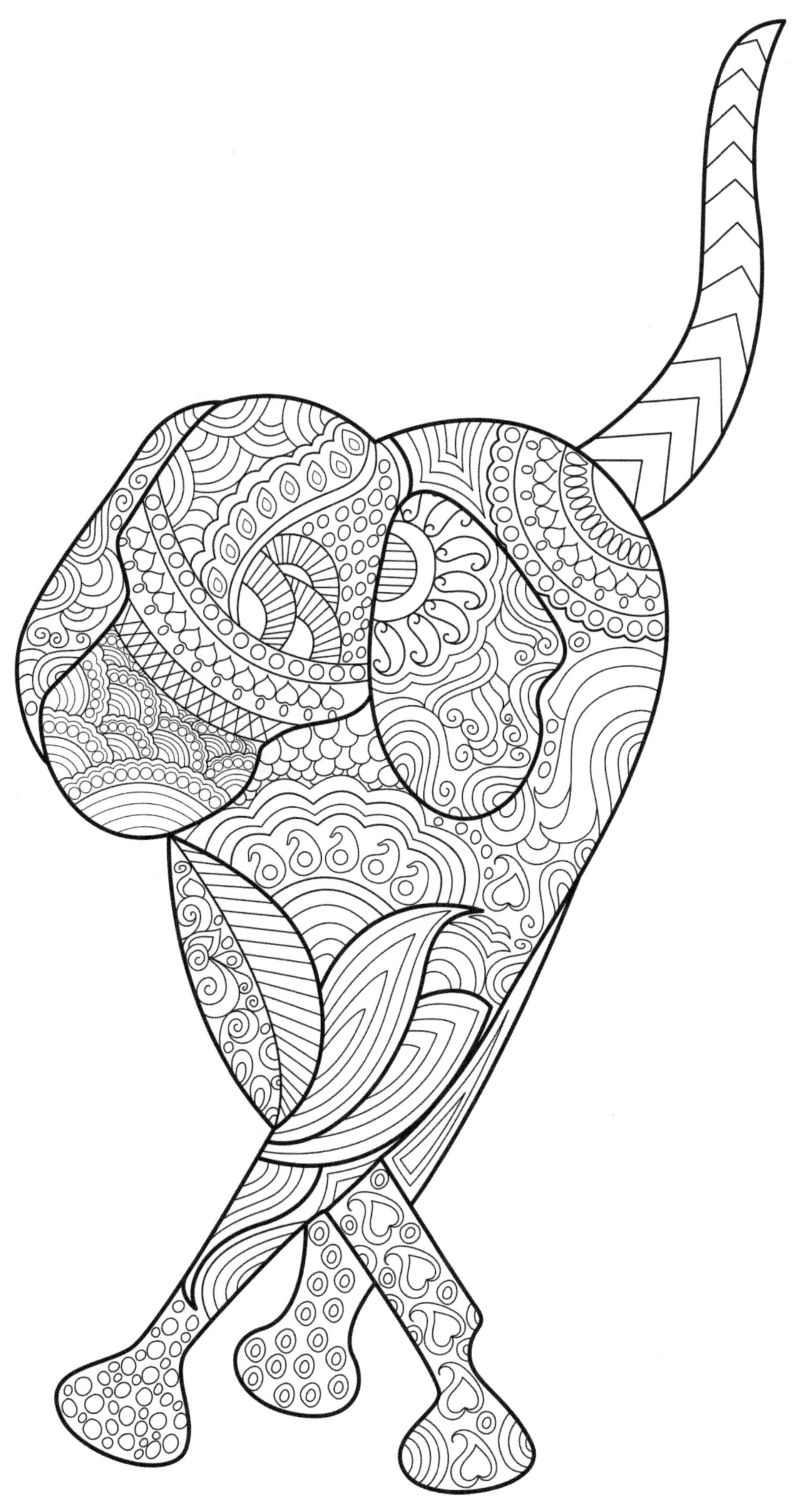

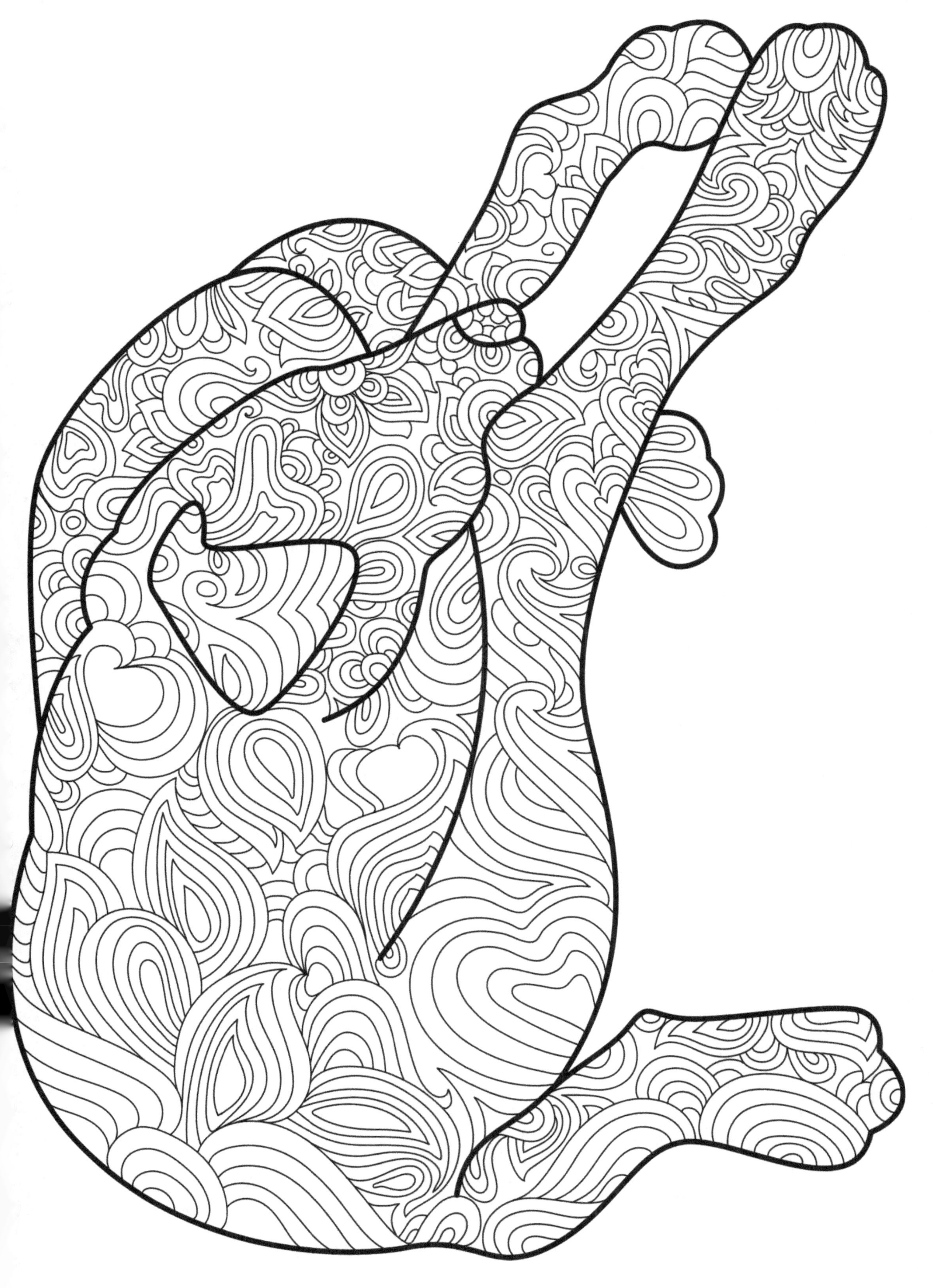

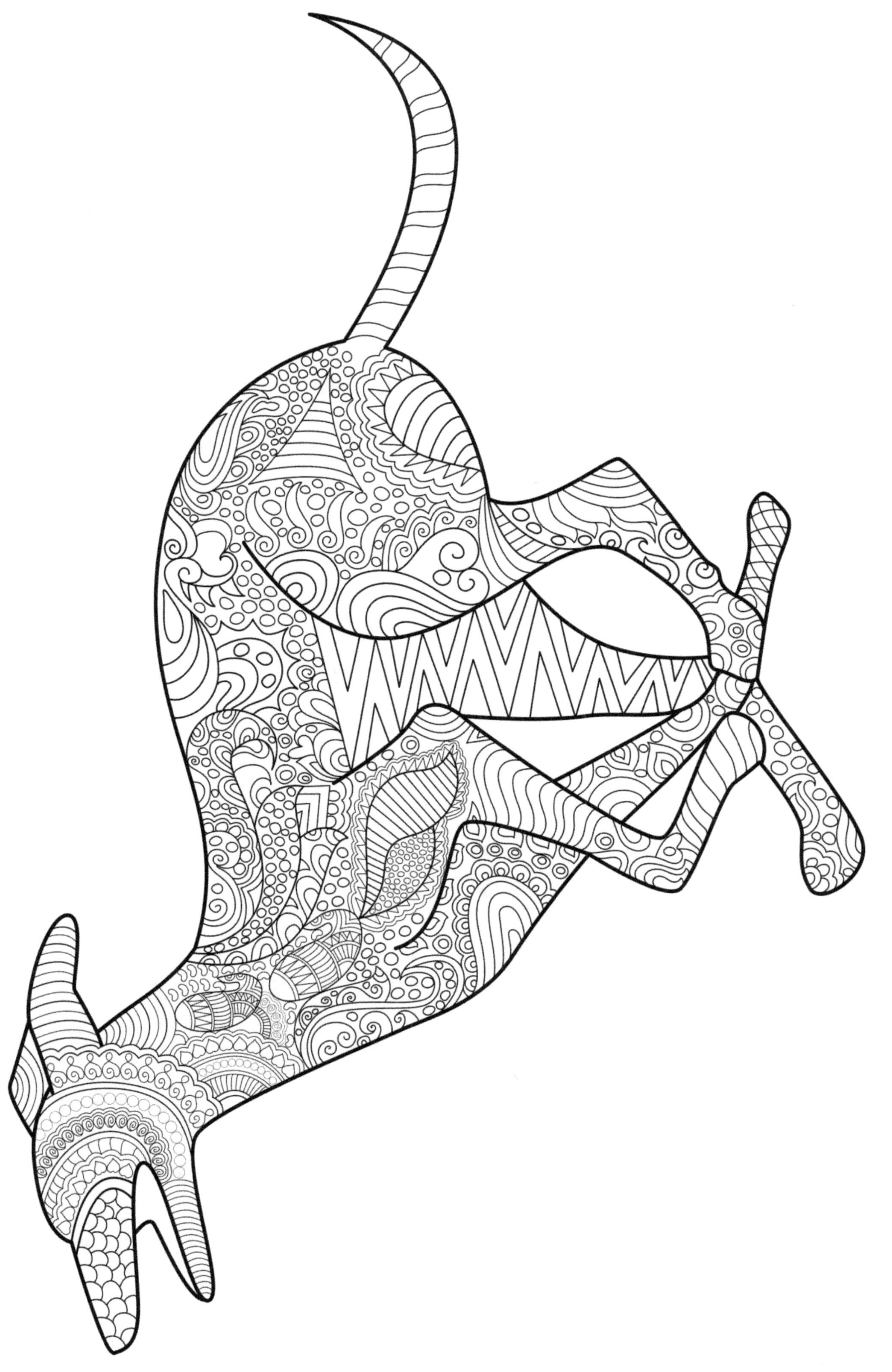

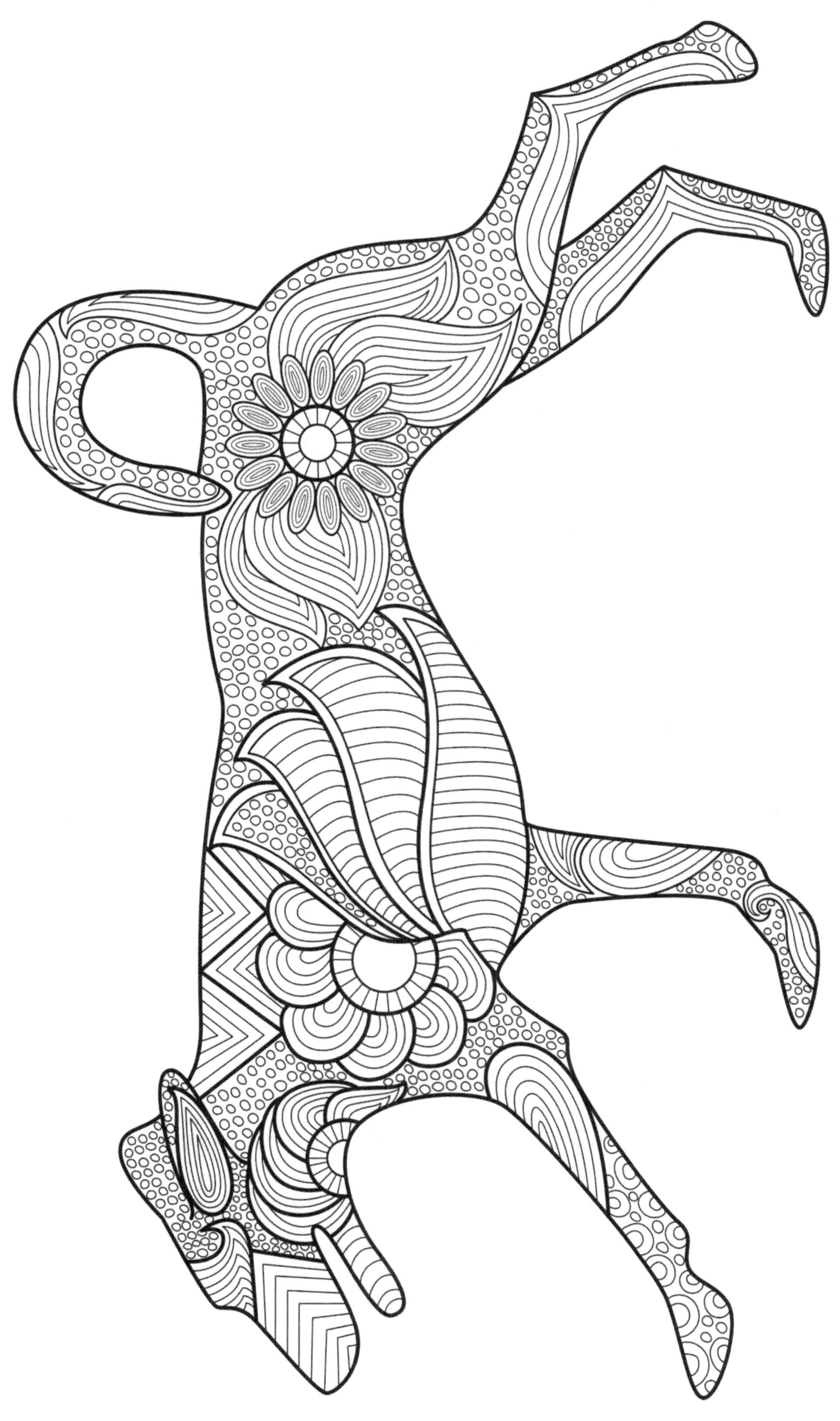

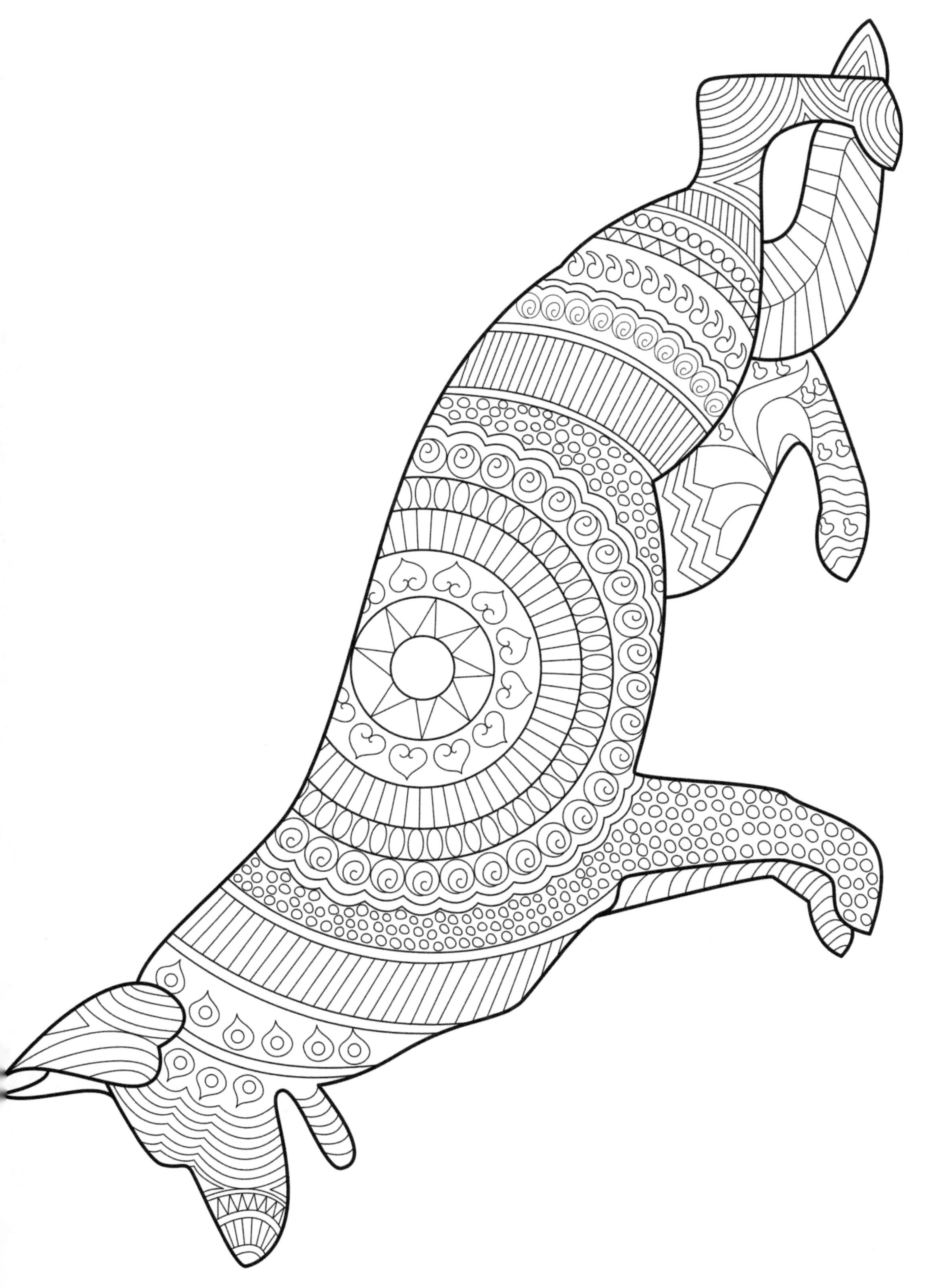

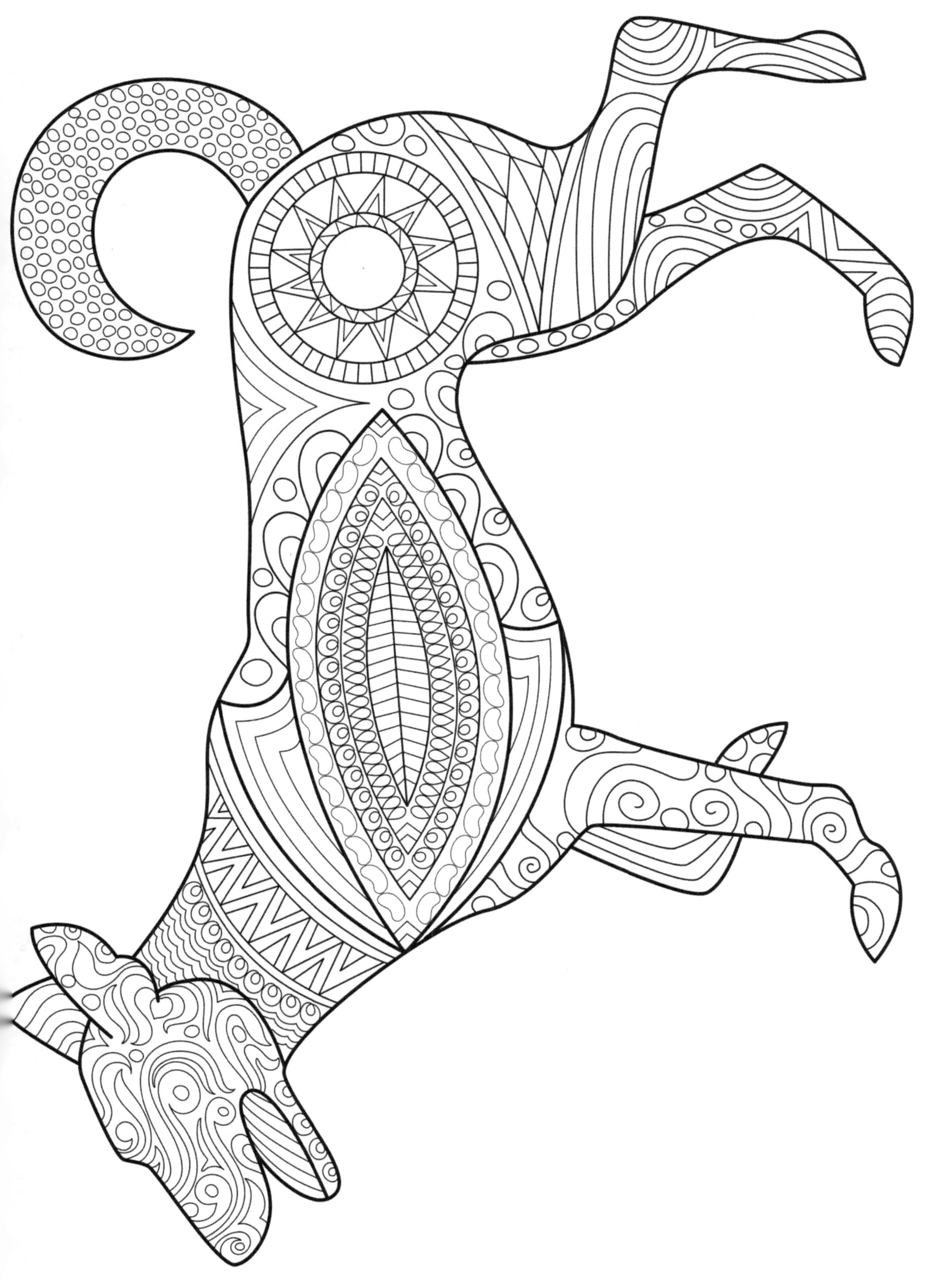

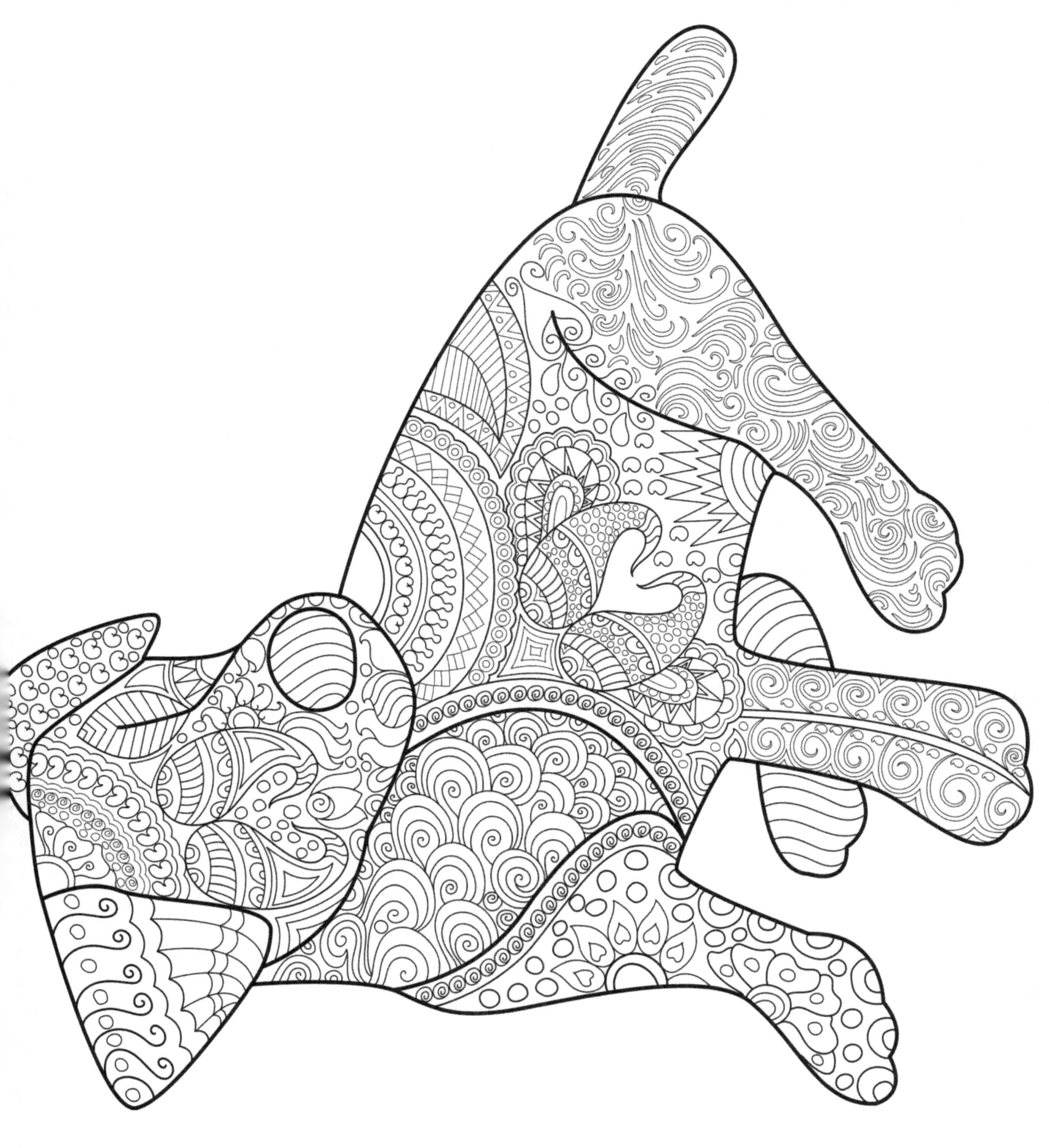

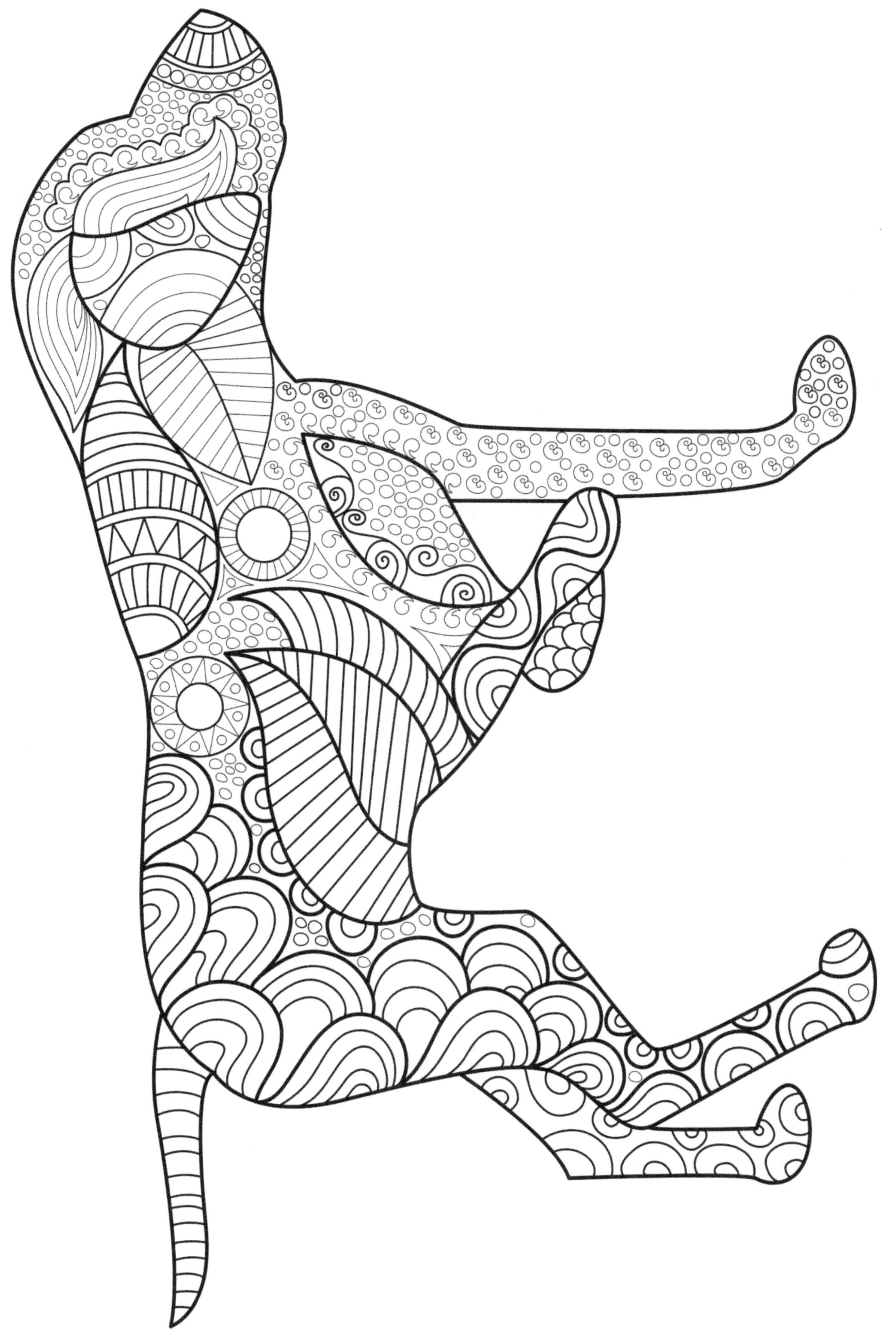

WE HOPE YOU ENJOYED THIS COLORING BOOK,
YOU CAN FIND MORE BOOKS ON OUR STORE.

Your Memories With This Book: